TO: ....

FROM: ....

TODAY'S DATE: ....

First Racehorse for Young Readers Edition 2023

Racehorse for Young Readers books may be purchased in bulk at special discounts for sales promotions, corporate gifts, fund-raising or education purposes. Special editions can also be created to specifications. For details, contact the Special Sales Department at Skyhorse Publishing, 307 West 36th Street, 11th Floor, New York, NY 10018 or info@skyhorsepublishing.com.

Racehorse for Young Readers is a pending trademark of Skyhorse Publishing, Inc.®, a Delaware corporation.

Visit our website at skyhorsepublishing.com

10 9 8 7 6 5 4 3 2 1

Editorial by Sam Hutchinson
Design and illustration by Vicky Barker

ISBN: 978-1-63158-717-7

Printed in China

My DADDY and ME

A KEEPSAKE ACTIVITY BOOK

WRITTEN BY
SAM HUTCHINSON

ILLUSTRATED BY
VICKY BARKER

FOR YOUNG READERS

This is my daddy!

STICK PHOTO
IN HERE!

His first name is ....

He is .... years old

This is me!

STICK PHOTO IN HERE!

My first name is ....

I am .... years old

My daddy's full name is

....

His date of birth is

....

He was born in

....

He has .... siblings

Was your daddy born where you live now?
Look up his place of birth on a map
... even if it is only a few streets away!

My full name is

....

My date of birth is

....

I was born in

....

I have .... siblings

Do you know where your name comes from?
Who chose it? Does it have a special meaning?
Design a badge all about your name.

My daddy's height is

....

His hair color is

....

His hair length is

....

His eye color is

....

Draw a picture of
your daddy!

My height is

....

My daddy is .... taller than me

My hair color is   My hair length is

....

My eye color is

....

Do you look similar to your daddy?
Do you have the same hair color?
How about your daddy's daddy
(your grandparent!). Do they look similar?

Draw a picture of yourself!
Make sure to sign your drawing,
like a famous artist.

The school my daddy went to is called

....

It is in

....

His favorite
lesson was

His least favorite
lesson was

....

Did your daddy do any
activities at school
or after school?
Write about them here.

....

....

....

....

Ask your daddy if he
has any photos or
certificates you can see.

My school is called

....

It is in

....

My favorite
lesson is

My least favorite
lesson is

....

Do you do any activities at school or after school?
Are they similar to the activities your dad did?
Write about a time that your daddy helped you
with something at school or after school.

....

....

....

....

During the school day,
when I am at school
or learning at home,
my daddy does

....

....

....

Stick a photo or
draw a picture here

Stick a photo or
draw a picture here

When daddy was my age
he dreamed of being a

....

....

....

When I am my daddy's age I want to be doing ...

My daddy's favorite color is

....

My daddy's favorite
piece of clothing is

....

Design a T-shirt
that you think
your daddy
will love!

My favorite color is

....

My favorite piece
of clothing is

....

Design a piece of clothing that
shows you and your daddy together!

Tell a funny story or draw a comic strip that will make your daddy laugh!

My daddy's favorite song is

....

The name of the band or the singer is

....

The song first came out in

....

My daddy loves this song because

....

....

....

My favorite song is

....

The name of the band or the singer is

....

The song first came out in

....

I love this song because

....

....

....

For breakfast, my daddy likes to eat

....

For lunch, my daddy likes to eat

....

For dinner, my daddy likes to eat

....

His favorite food is

....

His least favorite food is

....

He can cook .... really well!

Draw a picture here

For breakfast, I like to eat

For lunch, I like to eat

For dinner, I like to eat

My favorite food is   My least favorite food is

I can cook .... really well!

Draw a picture here

Using three different colors, circle words that describe you in one color, words that describe your daddy in another color and, in a third color, circle words that describe you both.

Kind

Funny

Silly

Serious

Outgoing

Fun

Clean

Confident

Friendly

Private

Quiet

Energetic

Caring

Calm

Thoughtful

My perfect day with my daddy would involve:

In the morning,

....

....

....

At lunchtime,

....

....

....

In the afternoon,

....

....

....

In the evening,

....

....

....

Draw you and your daddy together at the end of a happy day together! You can stick in a photograph if you prefer.

My daddy travels around by

....

Draw a picture of your daddy and his favorite mode of transportation.

When I am my daddy's age,
I will travel around in my

....

Draw a picture of your futuristic
mode of transport!

My daddy's favorite hobbies include:

....

....

....

....

....

STICK PHOTO
IN HERE!

My favorite hobbies include:

....

....

....

....

....

One thing we love to do together is:

....

One thing we would like to do together in the future is:

....

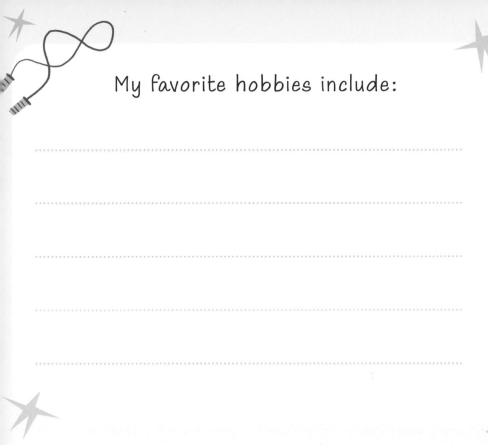

Finish writing this poem about your daddy!

I know my daddy loves me
He says it every day ...

....

....

....

....

....

....

....

....